"In poems that are as intense as they are lucid, Hai-Dang Phan illustrates James Baldwin's assertion that history is not the past, it is the present. The military hardware transported on the interstate, the vexing public memorials for past and recent wars, the refugees on the TV news, and the punk band named after the Viet Cong—Phan shows the present charged by the toxic continuing of the past. *Reenactments* is a book of haunted, forensic reckoning. Each poem in this beautiful and bitter book may begin in the intimate stories of the personal, but its ultimate scope is the national story of the broken American self and the havoc of its imperial project." —RICK BAROT

"Throughout this wonderful debut, we experience the various modes of reenactment: as memory, as mimesis, as fugue state, as cinema, and as translation. American English can no more turn away from what its Vietnamese citizens speak: 'I heard America burp.' Hai-Dang Phan, obsessed as he might be with the tenderness of survival and the transmogrification of war weapons, cannot forget that to be Vietnamese is also to remember Iraq and Syria. This book is greater than the interiority of family. It builds rooms in its stories to house more and more people." —FADY JOUDAH

"Haunted by the long aftermath of war and diaspora, Hai-Dang Phan's poems and translations explore how memory, like language, is never static. Moving from war reenactments to familial narratives to memories of Vietnam, Phan's language is pliable, attentive to terror, humor, sorrow, and hope. His gaze is clear-eyed and expansive. *Reenactments* is a gorgeously crafted, deeply moving, and singular debut." —EDUARDO CORRAL

"This must be the best poetry: the kind that makes you feel that you ought to appreciate your life, then change it, and urgently. Hai-Dang Phan writes what needs to be written, translates what we need to understand, and reminds me to love as much as I said I did. *Reenactments* deserves to go not just far, but beyond." —TARFIA FAIZULLAH

REENAC

TMENTS

POEMS & TRANSLATIONS

HAI-DANG PHAN

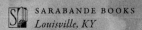
SARABANDE BOOKS
Louisville, KY

Library of Congress Cataloging-in-Publication Data
Names: Phan, Hai-Dang, 1980– author.
Title: Reenactments : poems and translations / by Hai-Dang Phan.
Description: First edition. | Louisville, KY : Sarabande Books, 2019.
Identifiers: LCCN 2018007358 (print) | LCCN 2018015333 (e-book)
ISBN 9781946448293 (e-book) | ISBN 9781946448286 (pbk. : alk. paper)
Classification: LCC PS3616.H37 (e-book) | LCC PS3616.H37 R44 2019 (print)
DDC 811/.6—dc23
LC record available at https://lccn.loc.gov/2018007358

Cover and interior design by Alban Fischer.
Manufactured in Canada.
This book is printed on acid-free paper.
Sarabande Books is a nonprofit literary organization.

  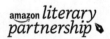

This project is supported in part by an award from the National Endowment for the Arts.
The Kentucky Arts Council, the state arts agency, supports Sarabande Books with state
tax dollars and federal funding from the National Endowment for the Arts.

FOR MY MOTHER AND FATHER

Maybe nothing ever happens once and is finished.

—WILLIAM FAULKNER

CONTENTS

I

Small Wars / 1

A Brief History of Reenactment / 2

For Fadhil Assultani / 4

To a Human Skull / 5

Video Elegy / 6

Get to Know Your Ghost / 8

Initial Encounter with Locals / 9

The Late Eddie Adams / 11

Of the 54th Massachusetts Regiment of Volunteers / 13

2

My Father's *Norton Introduction to Literature*, Third
    Edition (1981) / 17

Quiet Americans / 19

Spring Offensive / 20

At the Vietnam Center and Archive / 22

Fish in a Well / 24

How Many Islands / 25

Archive Fever / 33

Regarding the Spiritual and Social Situation of Vietnam Today
    (Observations That Are Current but Abstract and Highly
    General, Typical of the Deep, Sensitive, and Brave Souls
    of Poets) / 34

7504A Amarillo Blvd. East / 36

3

Email From Nguyễn Quốc Chánh / 39

Arrivals and Departures / 40

Saigon Notebook / 41

Crossing Hải Vân Pass / 42

Anniversary / 43

Kites / 44

Statue of the Century / 45

Lives of the Vietnamese Poets / 46

Elsewhere I Don't Know, but Here Must Be Different / 48

Blackout / 50

4

Osprey / 55

Self-Portrait with New Weapons Systems / 56

Motets from Florida / 58

Events Ashore / 60

5

Are Those F-16s? / 69

Watching *World War Z* / 72

Lunar New Year in Orlando / 74

March in Atlanta / 76

Greyhound, 1992 / 77

Waiting for al-Qaeda / 79

The Sorrow of War in Bloomington, Indiana / 83

My Viet Cong / 84

Ballistics / 87

6

My Mother Says the Syrian Refugees Look like Tourists / 91

Notes and Acknowledgments / 95

SMALL WARS

It was my turn to play dead, so I zipped up my flight suit
and monkeyed into the cockpit. Larry, Tobias, and Tim formed
the commando unit. Alfredo got the shaft again and played Charlie
all by himself. Wasting no time, they slipped back into the woods
like ghost soldiers and waited for the signal. Sunlight bombed
the forest floor. I pulled the pin on the smoke grenade, tossed it
under a tremendous wing, then slumped over my aircraft like a
    limp ragdoll.
In minutes, the shooting began. All hell broke loose, as planned.
Someone sprayed blanks into the enemy trees, laying cover for
    the others.
I could hear the branches and twigs snapping under the boots of
    my rescuers.
Someone radioed for helicopters and Phantom jets that would
    never materialize.
Pinecones dropped from great invisible heights. Black smoke seeped
into my eyes and blood rushed to my head and dangling arms.
A giant cicada singed the air with its emergency song, *too late too late*.
When I came to, the stars in my jungle burned like sodium flares.

A BRIEF HISTORY
OF REENACTMENT

On day one the photographer walks into camp
and immediately starts shooting. She shoots us

at breakfast eating our C rations, in our hammocks
reading *Stars and Stripes*. She shoots us in her sleep.

When we first cross paths at the creek, she says,
"Hello, Tiger! Nice combat boots. Is that thing *real*?"

pointing to my Special Forces jungle shirt.
"I'm afraid so," I say nonchalantly, trying to mask

my satisfaction. Day two: no more messing around.
The photographer has agreed to join the action.

"So what's the scenario?" A lone guerrilla left over
in a booby-trapped village jumps out of a hidey-hole

and ambushes the platoon on a search-and-destroy.
"Good thing I brought my black pajamas and sandals!"

What a trooper. She also plays the captured prisoner,
the native informant, and the beautiful turncoat.

The sniper girl is her favorite role because
it's like taking pictures. "The beauty, the beauty!"

Her voice volleys spookily from behind some rocks
as she picks off one of my men after another.

Sometimes the photographer shoots herself.
I know she has her own personal baggage—

later I find her sobbing in the bamboo grove.
I tell her it's okay, these wars only last three days.

"What will you do when it's all over?" she asks.
"I don't know," I say. "Plan the next one."

On day three, after another routine patrol, we sit
together on my favorite log, in the shade of oaks,

and devise more scenarios. The topo map
unfolds across our laps like a magic carpet.

She's got killer bangs above camera eyes.
I mark all the dangers and landing zones.

She speaks of controlled light and the hole
that opens up when you press the shutter button.

At twenty-four hundred our hands nearly touch.
There was a meteor shower. I call in mortar fire.

FOR FADHIL ASSULTANI

Round Hilla's date palms, first fruits glisten,
jeweled bracelets dangling from the arms of trees.

Mine was a silver maple, golden in the fall.
How far the winged seeds flew from my tree!

Black hawks hover low over groves.
The Euphrates obscured beyond the trees.

The stories about a gardenia and a girl who left
her shadow on the water you told to your tree.

In a pattern mimicking the flight of refugees
birds flee from the ancient city of trees.

Inside my pocket I carry a packet of seeds
carrying in their coats copies of trees.

Apricots are orange gifts. You call me Hadar.
Speak of your village and its hundred trees.

Tomorrow's another country where here will be
elsewhere, and I'll not know the names of the trees.

TO A HUMAN SKULL

from the Vietnamese of Chế Lan Viên

You belonged to someone!
In that dark theatre of bone,
do you still recall anything?
What dreams are showing?

Remember the killing fields?
Ten thousand heads cropped.
Or those nights your soul
leapt through the great fires?

On quiet afternoons do you
search for the trace elements?
Would you recognize your
soul if you bumped into it?

I must be losing my mind.
I just want to hold you until
your blood stains me
and infuses my sad little poems,

to bite you, tear you to bits,
swallow you, skull of my skull,
and enjoy whatever remains.
All these years blown apart.

VIDEO ELEGY

Your face did not rot
like the others.

They sent you back
nicely packaged,
cleanly and precisely

converted
into VHS. Forever

I will mourn
the record of your face,
personally

and professionally.
Don't worry,

they didn't miss a thing.
They got
you right after

and in the tub
for your last scrub.

They got you
putting on your suit
and messing up

your necktie. They even
got your sons

lifting you up
and sliding you into
a plastic bag

like a heavy goldfish.
Throughout, you

were more composed
than Buddha. They
got you dozing off

in your red cushioned box,
got the big procession

with all our family
dressed in ceremonial white.
They got you in the ground.

They got your face.
They got everything.

Its habits, eccentricities, fetishes;
whether it is free Saturday night
or Sunday afternoon for a visitation;
time of day, quality of light,
most likely to spook.
Mine looks like a lost salesman—
pink crumpled mouth above
frayed gray suit, and briefcase
bulging with the expired
driver's licenses of strangers.
Feed your ghost semifrequently:
plastic fruit will suffice,
preferably to scale and tropical;
buy flowers for it, fake ones.
Prepare a makeshift altar
with a most flattering portrait;
light some candles or incense;
mumble incomprehensible prayers.
Always, always remember
to throw your ghost parties
on the anniversary of its death.
Dress in white. Put on your sad smile.

INITIAL ENCOUNTER WITH LOCALS

Vietnamese Phrase Book, *Department of the Army pamphlet, 1962*

1.

Enter the village alone.

The password is _____.
Each individual must know these passwords.

Select the most able-bodied messengers.
Promise. Hurry. Swear.

We'll wait. All of you will wait.

2.

Come with me to the orchard.
Don't be afraid. We are friends.

Have a cigarette. Are you afraid?
Why? Of whom? What?

You certainly read our leaflets.

3.

What is the name of that mountain?

Which color is the most recognizable
from a distance? From what spot
could we have a better view?

What are the usual questions?
Who usually comes to this forest?

4.
We cannot see from here
what we wish to observe.

We need an open place—
a meadow, field, plateau.

It must be far away.
Do you know of any such place?

We will pay for everything.

5.
Point on the map.
We will call it the "drop zone."

Take care of this map.
We cannot give you another.

Here is my watch.
When shall we see you again?

Good luck.

THE LATE EDDIE ADAMS

for Michael Hofmann

Official combat photographer for the US Marines in Korea.
Arrived too late, damn it, to see combat;
instead, an assignment to cover the entire DMZ
—from end to end, a whole month
of barbed wire, guard towers, mountains, and mist.

Did three tours in 'Nam, more or less inconsecutively,
and embedded. *Semper Fi, baby!* Finally, saw combat.
Great rapport with soldiers, a grunt's grunt photographer.
Marine in flak jacket shaving in a trench at Khe Sanh;
baby-faced ARVN patrolling the jungle fog.

Pals with lieutenant general Lew Walt.
Free seats on choppers out of Da Nang. Hot spots.
Air-taxied in medias res, always armed and ready
with a Nikon—preferably three.
Bullets flying, he slowed down for faces:

helmetless, eyes like bayonets.
The Pulitzer he didn't want, he got. A reflex shot.
There was also his photo essay "Boat of No Smiles."
$100 of rice and gasoline secured him six days
aboard a leaky thirty-foot vessel crammed with refugees.

"It did some good and nobody got hurt."
Close-ups. Close quarters. Closer calls . . . Thirteen wars covered,
each was going to be his last. Then came *Life* and *Parade*:
US presidents (7), heads of state (65), Mickey Mouse (1);
Arnold Schwarzenegger (1) in a pool with a rubber ducky (1).

OF THE 54TH MASSACHUSETTS REGIMENT OF VOLUNTEERS

for Nate Klug

Gerald the Reenactor,
bespectacled and sweating under blue kepi cap
and replica sack coat, points his trigger
finger skyward at the lopped-off branches of the veteran elms—

"These very same trees stood here
for the dedication in 1897," he says,
the crownless centenarians rising up out of vaulted ground
like a pair of scarred arms without hands.

Posted in front of the Shaw Memorial all afternoon,
he's scholarly, avuncular, almost priestly,
with wooden musket, battered three-ring binder, and nylon gym bag,
personal effects of the Union dead.

For a Lincoln you can have a photo taken with him.
Hard, though, to picture him in battle as Sgt. William H. Carney
storming Fort Wagner, throwing down his gun,
seizing the flag like a spear, taking fire . . .

When a hop-on, hop-off tour bus pulls up
to the curb on Beacon, Gerald pauses midsentence,
head cocked, fact-checking bullet points
sprayed into a microphone by a pimpled sapling tour guide—

the first black regiment formed in the north,
the blue-blooded Bostonian Shaw who saw the war as a holy cause,
Augustus Saint-Gaudens's meticulous fourteen-year delay,
the models he hired for realism—

before launching back into his own lesson
about Carney, who saved the regimental colors,
Carney who received the Medal of Honor for his gallantry,
Carney who died from a freak elevator accident

while delivering a letter, there across the street . . .
Over his dust-and-pollen-coated shoulder the silent stomping
boots of the bronze soldiers still trample the air.
Dropped into the corner of the sculpture,

a pinecone and sprig of evergreen precede and follow history.
Next weekend he'll be in New Bedford,
where he—that is, Carney—was born slave and buried free man.
If Commander grants permission, he'll visit the grave.

Certain words give him trouble: *cannibals, puzzles, sob,*
bosom, martyr, deteriorate, shake, astonishes, vexed, ode . . .
These he looks up and studiously annotates in Vietnamese.
Ravish means *cướp đoạt*; *shits* is like when you have to *đi ỉa*;
mourners are those whom we say are full of *buồn rầu.*
For "even the like precurse of feared events" think *báo trước.*

Its thin translucent pages are webbed with his marginalia,
graphite ghosts of a living hand, and the notes often sound
just like him: "All depend on how look at thing," he pencils
after "I first surmised the Horses' Heads / Were toward Eternity—"
His slanted handwriting is generally small, but firm and clear.
His pencil is a No. 2, his preferred Hi-Liter, arctic blue.

I can see my father trying out the tools of literary analysis.
He identifies the "turning point" of "The Short and Happy Life
of Francis Macomber"; underlines the simile in "Both the old man
and the child stared ahead *as if* they were awaiting an apparition."
My father, as he reads, continues to notice relevant passages
and to register significant reactions, but increasingly sorts out

his ideas in English, shaking off those Vietnamese glosses.
1981 was the same year we *vượt biển* and came to America,
where my father took Intro Lit ("for fun"), Comp Sci ("for job").
"Stopping by Woods on a Snowy Evening," he murmurs

something about the "dark side of life how awful it can be"
as I begin to track silence and signal to a cold source.

Reading Ransom's "Bells for John Whiteside's Daughter,"
a poem about a "young girl's death," as my father notes,
how could he not have been *vexed* at her brown study /
Lying so primly propped," since he never properly observed
(I realize this just now) his own daughter's wake.
Lấy làm ngạc nhiên về is what it means to be astonished.

Her name was Đông Xưa, Ancient Winter, but at home she's Bebe.
"There was such speed in her *little body*, / And such lightness
in her footfall, / It is no wonder her brown study / Astonishes
us all." In the photo of her that hangs in my parents' house
she is always fourteen months old and staring into the future.
In "reeducation camp" he had to believe she was alive

because my mother on visits "took arms against her shadow."
Did the memory of those days sweep over him like a leaf storm
from the pages of a forgotten autumn? Lost in the margins,
I'm reading the way I discourage my students from reading.
But this is "how we deal with death," his black pen replies.
Assume there is a reason for everything, instructs a green asterisk.

Then between pp. 896–97, opened to Stevens's "Sunday Morning,"
I pick out a newspaper clipping, small as a stamp, an old listing
from the 404-Employment Opps State of Minnesota, and read:
For current job opportunities dial (612) 297-3180. Answered 24 hrs.
When I dial, the automated female voice on the other end
informs me I have reached a nonworking number.

QUIET AMERICANS

Kinnic and Mom in Đà Nẵng,
us in a frozen dinner aisle in River Falls.

*

Spooning our chicken vindaloo
we watch Mankiewicz's *The Quiet American*
on Turner Classic Movies,
something my father and I can agree on.

*

In a ditch near the watchtower
a Fiat bursts into a signal fire.

*

We aren't interested in the love
triangle or whodunit, but are spellbound
by old Saigon flickering in the rear window,
shadows of rue Catinet.

*

Snow puts the night on mute.
We know how it ends.

SPRING OFFENSIVE

It was time for an escalation.
The moles were brazen that year.
So my mother with a shovel for a spear
leveled their blind incursions

on her flower beds and veggie plot.
Little ugly volcanoes
belching black earth, those
molehills made her distraught

and our model lawn lumpy.
The neighbors appeared undisturbed,
and some even volunteered,
"The garden is looking lovely."

Two weeks into the campaign
erratic tunnels continued to trouble
the rose bushes—fallen petals
dyed the grass crimson.

Rain dripped from the million bells
the morning my mother found
her adversaries interred in the pond.
It was a slaughter, accidental.

Facing them at last, what shocked
her most were their flashy outsize hands,
their pinhole eyes hooded
and disappeared inside delicate skulls.

She retreated into a green shade
to watch the hummingbird zoom
like thought from bloom to bloom,
and hours off the daylily radiate.

AT THE VIETNAM CENTER
AND ARCHIVE

Lubbock, Texas

Between 1985 and 1987, he writes sincerely, gratefully
to the United Nations High Commissioner for Refugees,
the International Red Cross Central Tracing Agency,
Thai National Police, US Department of State, and more,
to no real end, though in quality each letter surpasses the last.

First he writes in Vietnamese longhand,
then someone helps translate and revise:
Don't say the boat was "stopped or encircled,"
say the boat was "surrounded" by the Thai pirates;
it's true they "took away with them eight girls in our boat,"
but "abducted" captures the situation better.

"The Reading Room will be closing in fifteen minutes."
I stare at the rust print left by a paperclip.
These are the letters of Mr. Nguyễn Văn Thể
concerning the disappearance of his granddaughter,
Đinh Thùy Trang, when she *escaped by boat* . . .

In the blue of his sentences a fishing boat leaves Vietnam,
on October 24, 1985, ventures into the South China Sea,
and drifts dangerously along the coast of Thailand.

I can just make it out, a small open V,
drawing its wake on the sea. *Around 9 A.M.*
of 26 October, the boat was surrounded
by five fishing boats belonging to Thai fishermen.

I recoil at these verbs—*invaded, searched,*
ransacked, pried, looked, seized: I see
teeth flashing inside mouths like knives.
No trace of his granddaughter Thùy.

FISH IN A WELL

from the Vietnamese of Phan Nhiên Hạo

When we were young my cousin
caught fish and fried them
some he dropped into the well
its water muddy and shallow
he said: "These are the lucky ones"

But every day
the metal bucket
plunged down dozens of times
I knew it must be hell
for the survivors

Around that same time my uncle still remained in a
    "reeducation camp."

HOW MANY ISLANDS

for my cousin Long

I.

I sit on the patio in the backyard of my cousin's house. I'm the guest. He's the cousin who is like an older brother. As I look out across the overgrown yard fenced by a wall of trees and the swimming pool covered since last summer, rainwater collected by its moss-green tarp makes a long mirror clouded with leaf litter, tree shadows, and bits of sky. The fern leaves floating on the surface arrange themselves into brittle continents, like an unfamiliar map of the world pulled down over an old school blackboard. That splash of orange daylilys, memories of my parents gardening. Hardy, adaptable, and effusive, the past blooms perennially, even in the most neglected plots.

We're back within the heat of early August in Minnesota. My cousin reappears with more cold beer. He lives with his family in a suburb just south of Minneapolis, not far from the airport where we landed many years ago, an August, too. We've spent two whole days together. Yesterday was a day of recreation, the two of us and his son biking around the lakes all afternoon. Today's the day for questions. I have many of them, but he needs only one to start. Cottonwood seeds, drifting from afar, alight on our bare feet.

2.

It was almost nighttime
when they finally made landfall—

he remembers stepping onto the beach,
everything blurred, everything
tilting, and looking back
at the black shape
resting in the shallow water.

He actually took in the boat
because it was dark
when they embarked, and over the water
he was tucked inside,

he remembers
the boat had eyes.

3.

When his mother asked
if he'd like to go to America with his uncle
he didn't even hesitate.
He was seven and liked adventures,

like exploring alleyways
until he was lost and had to find
a new route home.

Even after she explained
it would be long—
the trip—how large and scary

a thing the sea is.
Unlike rivers and lakes,

you can't see
to the other shore.

4.

Beached on the island,
there was this huge shipwreck.

Theories, rumors,
and origin stories swirled around
the ghost ship,

a steel carcass, a rust stain spreading
across the pristine sand.

Some people told him it belonged
to one of the refugees.
He wasn't so sure about that.

He ran around all day
with the kids he met in camp,
playing marbles.

The arrival of the supply truck was
always a red-letter day:
sometimes the aid workers would have toys.

"That's where I would get into those fights,
um, not really fights.

I would just get beaten up!"

It's in the family photo album,
his black eye in the black-and-white ID.

5.

Up in the jungle hills
there were swimming holes.
Waterfalls, lagoons, and rock-faced cliffs.

He was a city kid.
He couldn't help wondering
what the heck was in the water.

So he sat there and cried.
Eventually his uncle picked him up
and threw him in—

the other boys splashed around
the lagoon on floats
fashioned from bags or their own clothes.

6.

He remembers watching *Young Frankenstein*
on a big screen outside,
sitting on a hill with the others.

He wasn't scared or anything.
He could comprehend
without understanding
the language.

He remembers
laughing at the monster
doing his little dance.

Other things he recalls:
loving the Hi-C fruit drinks
but hating the cheese.

Instant noodles the night
his lips turned purple and blue
from the cold.

The fenced sky. An endless field.
Cars and motorbikes
flying by.

7.

Now he lives in a Minneapolis suburb,
not far from the airport
where we arrived years ago.

The swimming pool in the backyard,
unused since last summer,
a net for leaves.

"Local kids would say hi, ask me my name.
I didn't know what they were saying
so I'd just say *no*, because that seemed
safer than saying *yes*."

Daylily, spruce, sugar maple, scraps of sky.

His little boy stands
on the diving board, grinning and pantomiming.
He's a diver—no, a fish.

ARCHIVE FEVER

Last night dust storms
filled your sleep
with blinding debris—

letters from Amarillo,
the rustle of human voices,
bits of eros.

Now the sun's silver disc
begins its slow roll across the sky
like an epic hubcap.

In the cracked and blazing lot
you stand like a sundial
searching for that good shirt

you wear like someone else's life.

REGARDING THE SPIRITUAL AND SOCIAL SITUATION OF VIETNAM TODAY

(OBSERVATIONS THAT ARE CURRENT BUT ABSTRACT AND HIGHLY GENERAL, TYPICAL OF THE DEEP, SENSITIVE, AND BRAVE SOULS OF POETS)

from the Vietnamese of Phan Nhiên Hạo

Having lost our senses,
we carry on the struggle of cooking maggot corpses
from a busted refrigerator.

Mud dwellers, our goal in life
is to compete for the title
of The Filthiest.

Camped out in the gentlemen's club, chewing dog meat,
the worldly smart-asses talk big
then stumble home
to hang themselves upside down
in the style of bats.

Those shady dealmakers,
cunning malignant
clowns (who are rightly
scorned), travel in packs through the slums
plotting land grabs.

Hope is a gas station—
SOLD OUT.
Look at these few sorry daydreamers
pushing their scooters around
so tiresomely.

You fall through a door in the sky, stunned under hammered light and wasted powder blue. The road is cracked beyond repair. You turn toward the trailer park. Near the entrance someone is walking a dog. An abandoned dirt bike reminds you of the Schwinn a tornado once whisked away. Each car is a shipwreck. You try to step off the road but can't. So you just stand there, shadowless under ruined clouds. You turn and go, scrolling down the street. Click open a new path, leap to the other side of the Earth.

3

EMAIL FROM NGUYỄN QUỐC CHÁNH

from the Vietnamese of Phan Nhiên Hạo

Been in Đà Lạt
a week already
Sài Gòn was too hot
hotter than years past
I am more afraid of people every day
even the grass and trees looked a little fried.

Rained here yesterday
black clouds filled the sky
and flies coated the ground
inside a pho shop I asked someone
what's up with all the flies
he said it's fly season.

Cheers.

A passenger plane roars above us
like a password confessed in the sky.

I look down and around me—

impossible tangle of wires like knots of black hair,
streets bare and broken,

river choked with garbage,
the pastel buildings beside themselves

—when my cousin V. says
this must feel like flying.

We're standing on a second-floor balcony.

He must be imagining
patches of dead grass as lush green rice fields,

the only country he's ever known
dissolving in a solution of night.

I spot a stray dog.

It follows a memory to the corner
and lifts a hind leg into the air.

First stop, the Vạn Hạnh Buddhist University.
After a short meditation
the student monks race out of the hall
to catch the second half of a football match:
nil-nil on the green pitch of mindfulness.

*

Next attraction on the trauma tour,
site of Thích Quảng Đức,
the burning monk—I see nothing but dust,
a blur of bodies rushing in and out
of the street, sun igniting the horizon.

*

According to the vendors at Bến Thành Market,
the dead prefer US dollars to burn,
a paper Benz or Beamer, counterfeit
passports, fake plastic fruit and flowers.
In this, they resemble the living.

*

At New Noodle Heaven, my cousin and I slurp
our steaming bowls of soup, and stare
at new customers whose bedraggled uniforms,
shovels, and trumpets tell us they are fresh
from chanting mourning songs and digging graves.

Vapors rise from the South China Sea.
Ocean clouds. A ribbon of asphalt
          traverses a spur of the Annamite Cordillera.
   A motorbike inches up

   the bright face of the next mountain,
disappears around a bend, reappears at the sky's edge.
          The new tunnel shaves an hour off the trip to Huế,
     but we prefer the hairpin curves.

   Reaching the crest,
my family smiles at various cameras.
          Sun-dazed vendors scuttle out
     like startled crabs.

   I bought a tatty foldout map of Việt Nam.
On the long drive back down the spine
          of the coastal highway,
             its cheap ink rubbed off on my skin:

   a clutch of deforested hills
from the central highlands,
          a few razed villages,
     unpronounceable, all over me.

ANNIVERSARY

Bình Hưng Hoà Cemetery

Since your passing, we visit more frequently.
A dirt road slithers through a city
of headstones, makeshift stalls sell incense
and plane trees put out plastic bags.

Our prayers are perfunctory.
One of your sons dutifully uncoils a garden hose.
"Time to give the old man a bath."
Squalor of the living, splendor of the dead.

KITES

When one dive-bombed
I knew I was in another country
and out of sync with time.

STATUE OF THE CENTURY

from the Vietnamese of Trụ Vũ

I pound the pain of separation
into a statue for the park.
I'm going to call it
"The Soul of the Century."

My statue spills no tears—
they've all been spent.
My statue tells no stories—
what's the point now?

My statue: soul without
a halo above its head.
My statue: phoenixes
flamed out at its feet.

My statue stands naked,
erect, waving no banners,
casting shadows aimlessly,
looking out on nothing.

for Linh Dinh

Early on in his career, this poet wrote patriotic poems
inspiring youth to premature but glorious deaths.
This poet was one of the first of his countrymen
to cut his hair short and adopt barbarian clothing
and habits of speech. This poet spent three months
in jail, where he failed to commit suicide.
A reluctant survivor, he committed his poems
to memory. By his own admission, this poet
became brilliantly mad. He was, by all accounts,
the closest to a beatnik our country has ever produced.
To this poet, a finished poem is a corpse,
a published poem a mummy. Favorite themes:
romantic love, alcohol, and opium. This poet
was also a collector of jokes, many of them bawdy.
As critics have observed, this poet's poems—
profane, obscene, and silly—appear to be
written by a five-year-old or illiterate drunk.
This poet went from a somebody to a nobody,
and then back to a somebody nobody read.
This poet died in a neighboring country, of malaria,
while on a gold-digging expedition to escape from debts.
This poet introduced a cleaner, starker music
into verse and was the first to write about jazz.
Forgotten by all but a few, he escaped overseas.
This poet became obsessed with phantoms,

penning classics such as "Phantom Spring,"
"Adventures of Phantom," "Village of Phantoms,"
and "My Life as a Phantom." This poet is
the author of one unfinished historical novel
and over one hundred unwritten poems.

ELSEWHERE I DON'T KNOW, BUT HERE MUST BE DIFFERENT

from the Vietnamese of Nguyễn Quốc Chánh

Here in Phan Thiết.
It's seven o'clock.
The red sun flares.

Right now calm seas.
Right now sea full of algae.
Right now not so many swimmers.
Just a few people lying about, sitting, meditating.

A man, ragtag, legless, plays the superhuman
spinning round and round on his veined pole.
(He looks like he's survived from centuries ago
not unlike those invalids of a million shipwrecks.)

Elsewhere the sea is salty, at times bitter, but here
the sea is sublime with the scent of fermented fish.

The history of the sea is inevitable, everywhere war,
but here the sea is completely different.

Elsewhere the sea dreams of uniting all at once
her islands to her aging continents.

But here the sea dreams eternally of bottled fish sauce.

That's why here, all over the place, all the time, it smells funky.

BLACKOUT

in memory of Trần Thị Thu

The subzero weather and cryogenic freeze
of your bedroom is your last bid at immortality.
The air conditioner produces an arctic breeze
in this corner of Ho Chi Minh City.

Like a sunbather on a ocean liner,
you doze on the throne of your folding chair.
Arrayed on a tray are "Western" painkillers,
sleeping pills, and black dye for your hair.

I sit beside you, grandson and honorary guest.
Korean soaps play on the television all day,
prepaid for your voluntary house arrest,
dubbed so you can understand what they say.

The karaoker next door stops midcroon—
the electricity has been cut
for the blackout on Monday afternoons.
I fan you so you don't melt.

Your life stretches across three wars.
Your mother was slain by bandits near the village
where you were born. You disobeyed your father
and fell in love with a poet at a young age—

the one who went north for the August Revolution,
who called on fall to block the coming spring.
This romantic version is your historical revision.
Your name means autumn.

You were married off that spring.

Swelling out of the ocean like a bad feeling,
heard before seen slouching toward Miramar
over Venice Beach, it's the Bell Boeing V-22,
not sleek but versatile, able to launch
from al-Asad, fly to Mudaysis, perform pickup,
then return, all within the golden hour,
fast enough to outrun a difficult past,
the budgetary hurdles and crashes in R&D,
the $72 million price tag, flyaway,
its many modes, and we think moods;
you remember its namesake in another state,

fled from some outer dark, gliding above
the diamond, from left field to center,
where it made its home up in the stadium lights,
a crown of wooden swords for its nest,
hovering in the swampy air like forethought
as the crack of a bat sent a tiny moon
into orbit, a wave rippling through
the crowd, the lights on their tall stems
powered on, day powered down,
and you had no team, you did not know
whom to root for, home or away.

SELF-PORTRAIT WITH NEW WEAPONS SYSTEMS

You used to be thirty, now you're something.
Treat. Yo. Self. Cloths, fragrances, massages,
Mimosas, and fine leather goods. This year let's try
Not to kill our plants again. My voicemail
Called to tell me I am running out of memory.
At the scene of Qaddafi's capture, a Yankees cap.
I reserve the right to unlike this. On a scale of 1 to 10 . . .
Her blouse forgets nothing. A text declares *i'm here!*
Yesterday is my alibi. The sky five minutes before midnight.
Suddenly everyone wants to talk about unicorns.
At least you share a birthday with Snoop Dogg.
That recent post on drones was a real downer.
Your morals will be supported. The new Hummingbirds
Will buzz into rooms, drop a payload, and leave.
A scar invited a touch. Apply gentle pressure
When braking. Do something painful each day,
Like brushing your teeth. Air the night collected
Cools these rooms. The brass is already talking
About future engagements. I am a little bit happier
Than I was a moment ago. Hold steady
While I take the temperature of your voice.
You cannot doubt the lemon cake. The eurozone
Is really just Sarkozy and Merkel. Sometimes, Cameron
Will throw his two cents in. We talk of our lives
As if we were others. With an ear to the air
The birds have organized. Considerable cloudiness

With occasional rain showers. When I say tomorrow
I mean an expression of regret. Today is nothing
Like 1980. Let's put the future behind us.
I'll walk you just as far as this thought.

The sun here is democratic. It burns everyone.
My body tells my mind August was overheating, asking for
    a sudden downpour.
September, a walk under what look at first like weeping willows.
Moss garlands the great oaks, gargantuan limbs across
    darkened streets.

*

A sparrow sails down from the sassafras
to collect blades of grass for hurricane-ready housing.
    On this side
of the sunbaked municipal building, the weathered wall lies exposed.
A sawed-off drainpipe sticks out of brick
    like a raw bone.

*

Downtown, the tables of the pool hall glow in the losing afternoon.
Your voice wells up from the cellular phone,
    unconsoled,
but not unforgiving. Our weekly fight is interrupted
by a coughing air conditioner and the high-pitched screeching of a
    passing car.
    This time I mean it.

*

What do the clouds have to say that they can never remember?
A forgotten memory of their Atlantic crossing?
    The earth
is the same earth, but different. On the shoulder of evening,
lifted by palm trees, the moon still rises—
    half-emptied.

The sea a blue prairie waving at me.
The sky rewriting its history of clouds. A triangle of light
    advancing. Between the sky that is blue

and the sea that is blue, the smoking islands
    floating like ships. The ships.
Black, flinty, right out of Homer. Rendezvous on a beach

    between hovercraft and tank,
the empty beach scored with swirling track marks.
    The two figures, soldiers, strolling like lovers,

armed and ready. The gray tide
    attacking an idea of the shore.
The exhilaration of attack, the melancholy of retreat.

    The many greens, the blues. All kinds of blue.
The blue of flags. Blue metallic skin etched with blue insignia.
    My blue nights, my blue days.

Cloudlets. Cloud shaped like a frigate. Frigate cloud.
    Clouds general. Perforated, striated, puffy.
Apocalyptic cloud kicked up by rotor blast of a Sikorsky

    like a thick black curtain drawn
over the staging ground, bloodless landscape
    in which the theater occurs. A would-be bomb in full bloom.

Landscape with howitzers. Landscape with unmarked airplane,
    trucks and jeeps deployed for earthquake relief.
Light infantry and heavy artillery.

    The village kids out on reconnaissance.
The local flora and fauna. The white plumes
    of shocked wavelets fanning out

in the wake of the amphibious assault on the beachhead.
    The glassy creek hiding
in the golden meadow, the sleepy foothills

    nodding in the distance. The men wading into real fields
of tall grass, ambushed by daylight. The men
    exchanging fire with their sham enemies.

The sensuous, gentle cows watching from behind the shrubbery.
    Three Black Hawks resting on the grass runway,
blades bowed under the soft light over the bay.

    The angel angles. If I had to guess
where the camera was positioned,
    I'd say somewhere in the back of my head.

My eyes, twin planets. Each morning
    I arrange myself in a pattern of looking,
decide what part of the horizon to face,

feel the volumes of air
moving through the frames of these establishing shots,
        light works, and cloud studies.

Bands of sunlight striping a bleached horizon
        of date palms and minarets, an eggshell-blue sky
stacked atop a thin green line of trees,

        creamy white sandbanks of the Suez
running alongside the USS *Dwight D. Eisenhower*,
        Egypt sliding past.

A childhood obsession with military aircraft
        helps me to identify the Hornet in the corner
and the Seahawk pinned like a specimen.

        Airplanes nosing into position,
tipped and alert like nipples.
        The webbed landing gear of the Canada goose

and a bird's nest of concertina wire.
        What I think is a Canada goose is actually
a weathervane. What I think is a toxic

        Minotaur born from biological warfare
is just one man hiding another, a hulk wearing a gas mask
        sprouting what looks like a mutant leg,

pieces of protective equipment littering the chemical ground.
      Water of our beginning, water of our end.
The green screens glowing with data. The surfaces hot with incident.

      The deadpanned portraits.
The blonde in technical gear radiating tranquility
      like a blue-eyed Madonna, framed by folded jet wings

carrying the rolled missives of missiles,
      her grease-stained fingers
clutching black gloves, her brown shirt emblazoned

      with a wolf's head and bearing the name GRACE.
"Married to the Sea" tattooed in running script
      along the bicep and forearm

of the cupid-faced, crew-cut sailor.
      What's your name? Where are you from?
Codes, call signs, numbers, flags. So many flags.

      Helmets and goggles. Vests and cargo pants.
Gunmetal-gray folding chairs arrayed on a sea-foam-green floor.
      The monk in saffron robe

sitting next to the soldier wearing steel-blue digital cammies.
      Spiffy midnight-blue jumpsuits,
oily wetsuits annoying to take off,

pink parkas in Antarctica,
and the distressed jeans of the civilian at the harbor terminal.
Roll call. Target practice. Cigarette break.

Clearing tripwires, manning the rail, tending
to a goat in Panama, skinning snakes in Indonesia,
washing down the superstructure with fresh water

and scanning the flight deck for foreign objects.
This is a warm-up exercise, my morning ritual in dark times,
the pages of the orange notebook filling

and filling with everything I see—a tracery of flight paths,
wave forms,
tread marks—and even more I cannot face.
Accumulation and attrition. The clouded

black surface of the carrier deck. All the platforms.
Fighter planes the color of rain, ghosts, and amnesia.
At the edge overlooking the Pacific,

five men standing inside the outlines of five human-shaped targets.
Mercy, a hospital ship off the coast
of Vietnam, and *Justice*, a camp at Guantánamo Bay.

We're big in Japan, Ghana, Indonesia, Haiti.
We're somewhere in the North Arabian Gulf.
We're back in Đà Nẵng. We can be ready in under an hour.

At the ends of the earth. The sea again,
    glimmering opera for optic nerves, a glitter bomb
spilling sequins in the millions.

    Daily, nightly, along the shores of light,
the events that will not end, and have only just begun.
    The horizon.

5

ARE THOSE F-16S?

Iowa I-80

Mid-March, winter's casualties
still litter the roadside,
burnt carcass of a jackknifed semi,

abandoned cars sprouting
little flags. Disaster flowers,
and false rumors spread

of spring. This interstate
makes a philosopher out of you,
accelerating into the glare

eastbound on the Mixmaster.
"125 Traffic Deaths This Year.
Get Your Head Out Of Your Apps."

Velázquez's *Christ Crucified*
on a four-story Clear Channel billboard,
his commuted illuminations.

"The F-16 is going to die out,"
says Vice Commander Kevin on air.
Who will man the Reapers?

Sometimes even the sun
can elevate your terror to new levels,
the color orange,

as the last thin mists of fog burn fast
through the dark-green archipelago of trees
you speed past. Drifting

into the slipstream behind
another big rig hauling
the pristine hugeness of a turbine blade,

you contemplate
the functional beauty of a giant's wing,
how you, too, tilt at windmills.

"Fields of Opportunities"
is the state motto,
but you desire just one.

Are we there yet?
asks your life awake again
in the passenger seat.

Decelerate as the new gun factory
swings into view, its gleaming windows
and meandering supply roads.

Was it Rilke who said to "live
the questions now"? We have so much
to live for, careering forth

into the assembly
of the present, emergency
lights flashing.

WATCHING *WORLD WAR Z*

for my sister Kinnic

Remember when Dad said he killed zombies
for a living? Thanksgiving, we were all
downstairs watching *World War Z*, Brad Pitt
stabbing every undead soul with the kitchen
knife he had duct-taped to the end of a shotgun,
as he led his family to the tenement rooftop
in Newark where, of course, a helicopter awaited.
Outside, trees stood sentry and winter threatened
to launch its first assault on our nights and days
while another city succumbed on the plasma screen
and death was figured as an unwanted rebirth.
Which is when Dad deadpanned the thing
about killing zombies at work and we laughed
in the dark not knowing what a botnet was.
Shortly after, you were the first to go,
though you lasted longer than anyone expected,
lumbering back upstairs to sleep just before
a tidal wave amazed the walls of Jerusalem,
aided by computer-generated imagery
of the different shapes a crowd can take:
pyramid, tentacle, wave. The world,
for the most part, resembled ours. After all,
ours is an age of extremity, zombie sci-fi
reflecting and allaying our worldwide anxiety.
Or so Susan Sontag would say, whom

I refrained from quoting because I anticipated
your eyes rolling, "There he goes again."
You also missed Mom's live commentary
on the chaotic scene at the besieged airport:
she said it was just like Saigon, April, 1975,
the runway swarming with desperate bodies,
the improbable escape on the last flight out.
It must have happened in ultra–high definition,
those final days before they were Mom and Dad.
The movie family was reunited in Nova Scotia,
svelte in parkas and ready to face the sequel.
That was November 2013. We were at your house
in Madison celebrating Thanksgiving early.
Another war was on.
You were about to be a mother
and slept for a generation.

LUNAR NEW YEAR IN ORLANDO

Cumulonimbi big as battleships
pour rain and hail on the fleet
of Hondas and Toyotas parked pell-mell
at the Central Florida Fairgrounds.

It's the Year of the Dragon.
Look who showed up again to the celebration.
It's your past, all decked in festive militaria.
Next to a piece of heavy artillery,
the peach blossom passes out little red envelopes,
filled with lucky money, we hope.
A young family in matching camo tees
says *cheese* to the iPhone aimed at them.

Before long, you are pulled away
by short, round men in full dress whites,
their pants taken out by their tailors,
as their wives take Mom hostage.
On the drive over, I was already
looking forward to it all being over.

The sky's ceasefire sends me outside
to the damp pitch where I kill time
chatting with the freckled teenaged merchant
who sells expired candy and tasteful weaponry.
Small arms fire breaks out nearby:
a squad of boys runs, brandishing new

plastic automatics—his toy guns are a hit.
They sing oddly like the birdsong
I woke to this morning.

Soon after, I spot you by the Swift Boat,
a PCF-171 propped up on stilts,
stranded on the grass like a desolate shipwreck,
the first one you've seen since the war,
when you patrolled arterial waterways
of the Mekong Delta, slicing through
the dream work of emerald jungles,
into nightmares in broad daylight, past floating
villages you'll never see again . . .
You pat its side like an aluminum horse,
gunmetal skin reflecting nothing,
and look at me with an expression
that could have been a smile.

Skipping Miss Vietnam of Florida,
we rescue Mom, retreat in the rental car,
and spend the rest of the day peacefully
on your old Navy friend's patio,
picking through the rubbishy aftermath,
watching for the real gator
in his fake pond.

MARCH IN ATLANTA

from the Vietnamese of Phan Nhiên Hạo

I don't recall the color of March,
only the snow melting that day in Chicago.
I flew south to Atlanta,
walked around a sparkling downtown
circled by dismal districts.

Setting out, I explored the monotony of manhole covers,
observed the immature flies of spring,
nervous vibrations atop pathetic flowerpots,
in front of a liquor store dotted with cigarette butts.

I knew an incident just occurred
but didn't see any blood.
I bought a map to make things clear.
You are here, an outsider.

In the Coca-Cola museum,
I pissed more than I drank
of the different sodas
tricking my thirst.

I heard America burp.

GREYHOUND, 1992

from the Vietnamese of Phan Nhiên Hạo

In '92 I crossed the country,
from Atlanta to Seattle, by bus.
I had $300 and about that much English.
Over the flat fields of the Midwest
I saw cows crowded like ants.
The air smelled like shit for miles and miles.
The locals seemed unfazed.
Had I lived there long enough,
I wouldn't smell anything either
I guess.

Many black folks rode the bus.
Only later did I learn it was the easiest way
for poor people to travel state to state.
They have lots of time and little money.
In the restroom of a transfer station in Denver
a white kid offered me a joint and something else.
That was also the first time I saw an Indian
not from a movie. He was too drunk
to remember what tribe he belonged to.
He didn't carry a gun or bow,
but held a tall boy while slumped in a corner.
I turned down the joint and something else to avoid
becoming a yellow man who exists only in a movie.

I sat beside a Hmong dude—shorter than me!

This guy drank milk the whole trip.

You might have thought he was a loser

hoping for a second growth spurt.

But I know why he guzzled so much milk:

basically, his stomach hurt.

I, too, suffered from gastritis once.

The result of years of starvation

and bitterness from growing up in a piss-poor nation.

He clutched the jugs (Made in the USA, 75 cents)

like a pair of fake breasts you toss in the trash after sucking.

Back then, I felt like an immigrant made from plastic,

resilient and resistant to all types of acids.

In 1992, the Greyhound from Atlanta to Seattle

only cost $85 for the 2,600 mi. journey.

America, you swallowed me down your throat,

cheaper than dirt.

Walking down Broadway today
I get a call from my old neighbor
I haven't heard from in ages.
"Hy-Vee is having a sale on soda."
That's too bad because New York
is so expensive. She's always
wanted to see the city, but knows
she won't, "not in this lifetime."

I recall well our first meeting.
She wore a unisex cherubic
helmet of tight crunchy curls,
a giant sweatshirt declaring
for the record the season
(Cyclones vs. Hawkeyes)
and the state we were in:
A House Divided!

Local, daunting, heavyset,
thick-skinned, and windswept,
she was a high-functioning
schizophrenic. For years,
a medical transcriptionist until
an episode left her jobless, bereft.
I was a low-functioning poet.
We became good neighbors.

Our communicating hallway
was a dimly lit echoey channel
of humdrum broadcasts.
Often I tuned in for company.
She had the isolato's talent
for talking to herself. Her laugh
swept the floor, her curses
brightened the corners,

and her humor was Kevlar.
Of our absentee landlord
Cheryl: "Total B-I-T-C-H,
all caps, scary letters";
of her chronically teary cat:
"Poor Miles has herpes,
but you don't have to worry
unless you're also a cat."

Some days were too much.
When her Ziploc gallon bag
of laundry quarters disappeared
she called the cops, who called
Cheryl in San Luis Obispo . . .
She had until New Year's Day
to find a new place and move out.
"Merry-fucking-Christmas."

I came over one day to help,
the only time I ever stood inside
her apartment. Above the table

Mia Hamm with a flying ponytail
executed the poster-perfect
corner kick; in the only photo
on the fridge, a girl in shadow
calmly stroked a kitten—

"I keep that to remind myself,
'You weren't always ugly.'"
She showed me the pantry,
where a shocking stockade
of perished nonperishables
towered on unstable shelves.
Freed from the great wall
a warped can of beans fell

and rolled to a stop at my feet.
A dud. We exploded into laughter.
"Those date back to the time
I was waiting for al-Qaeda."
Under the kitchen sink
she still kept a blaze orange
backpack, her Walmart
terrorist attack survival kit.

"Do they kill the virgins first
or keep us as trophies?"
She felt woefully unprepared
for what was to come.
Failing to find an answer,
I made eyes with July's

Cosmo pressing luridly against
a see-through storage bin.

The surf of traffic washes
our rooms away. I still don't
know what to say, so I promise
to send her a postcard, and do:
an aerial shot of Central Park
in autumn, something someone
might see flying into the city,
their feelings in fall colors.

THE SORROW OF WAR IN BLOOMINGTON, INDIANA

after Bảo Ninh

Forgotten by peace,
all day and all night
the water streams

into the embrace
of the coarse undergrowth
and wild grasses.

The humid atmosphere
condenses, its long moist,
chilly fingers sliding

in and around.
The stream moans.
A sea of fire

enveloped them.
Blown out of their
shelters. Bodies.

Backs, flowing.
Crows darkened the sky.
The rainy season.

At the bookstore where we like to go, my lover finds me
an almanac of the war, knowing all about my obsessions.

*Viet Cong was a derogatory term for Vietnamese Communists
in the south. Instructed by Hanoi to lie low until 1959, they*

*were activated by the North Vietnamese Politburo to begin
a guerrilla war in the south in an attempt to subvert and overthrow . . .*

Viet Cong was also the name of this post-punk band from Calgary.
They sound like lasers drilling into ice, winters in Wisconsin,

my heart's furnace. *The sound that begins* Viet Cong *resembles someone
trying to punch their way out of a coffin*, according to Pitchfork.com.

In Saigon once, my grandmother's caretaker silently clapped
her hands over her ears, mouthing "Bomb! Bomb! Bomb!"

"Three" was what everyone called her. "Bomb"
was the only English word I heard Bà Ba speak.

When Three was a girl the sky opened up with Rolling Thunder
so loud she became partially deaf. War loaned her the word.

My nickname, Bờm, when you say it, sounds like a little bomb.
My American classmates couldn't say it right, so I became "Boom."

But I was talking about Viet Cong. The band came under attack,
for not knowing two syllables could trigger such a grim

history. During rehearsal, the bassist aimed his guitar
like a machine gun. "All you need is a rice paddy and straw hat,"

the drummer shouted. "That would be so Viet Cong!"
Their new name is Preoccupations.

As a kid, I watched every single Vietnam War movie.
Apocalypse Now. The Deer Hunter. Full Metal Jacket. Platoon.

You name it. I was too young to realize I was after
my own face on the NVA soldiers and VC guerrillas.

I hummed along as King, the black soldier played by Keith David,
sang low, "I come from Alabama with my banjo on my knee,

and I'm going to Louisiana, my true love for to see. Oh, Susanna!"
Back then, I didn't know they shot the war in the Philippines.

Mount Makiling for jungle scenes. Cavite for river and village scenes.
Or that Vietnamese refugees were hired to act various roles, like VC.

About the worst thing my parents can call anyone is *Việt cộng*.
It's been years since anyone has called me "commie," or "gook,"

or "chink." One was Kevin, the other Steve. Both redheads.
On the school bus home, Kevin slurred, "Go back to your own
    country!"

My friend Shaun saved me that day from a black eye.
If you're wondering, I come from the Midwest of Everywhere.

Hai-Dang means "lighthouse." Like the painter in the novel
I have had my vision. A visible signal of safe harbor

or mark of danger. Call me mariner or renegade or outcast.
My lover and I have names for each other we keep like secrets.

Once upon a time, there was a man who, freed from one
prison, found himself released into a still vaster prison.

Inside he was determined to escape. But first
had to devise a plan, come up with an alias.

He paid for fake ID, pretended to be secretly Viet Cong.
And if they asked him for his name he'd give them mine.

BALLISTICS

In a ballistics lab in Maryland
three artists known as The Propeller Group
aimed assault rifles at each other
and fired them simultaneously into gel blocks

constructed to resemble human flesh.
Fragments of the projectiles,
fused on impact, float suspended
around a flower of smoke. Shot through

with light, the resulting twenty-one gel blocks,
like this one elegantly displayed
inside a custom vitrine, enchant. On a flat screen
hanging on the wall like a black canvas,

the collision replays on a single-channel loop
in extreme slow motion, the bullets
tearing the surface of the seen
as when a lake breaks from a stone.

The AK-47 vs. The M16 was on view
at the Des Moines Art Center that Thursday evening
back in early June when I visited
"one last time" with you.

Little cloudbursts we left on the glass:
pierced flower, bright insects, tiny supernova.

I stopped looking—you were there.
We turned and walked away.

MY MOTHER SAYS THE SYRIAN
REFUGEES LOOK LIKE TOURISTS

because she has just finished telling the story of our escape
and needs to draw a comparison, return us safely to the present,

December 2015, we're back at my sister's childproofed house,
keeping warm by winter sun, central heating, and our sweatpants;

because some do: "Ghaith joyfully snapped selfies, the Aegean
glimmering in the background. He looked much like a tourist,"

suggests the reporter at large in the *New Yorker* article I read
about one refugee's epic escape from Syria, and think of again

when my mother can't make room in our story for more people;
because my mother never quite has the right words in English,

though to be fair, she said "travelers," and seemed anxious after;
because she's not callous, you must understand, just protective . . .

In the blue porcelain bowl on the granite-top kitchen island
where we gather faithfully around my mother and the story,

there are three balls of white rice shaped like warm eggs,
and a fourth, forming in her hands, being pressed into service

as she recounts making them before, wrapped in banana leaves
and secreted inside pockets. These are for my nephew, Aidan,

who loves rice like he loves Cheerios, who will be hungry
once his toy train runs off too many tracks, and who just turned

two, around the age I was when we left, a coincidence my mother
points to like a storybook illustration . . . It's December 1981.

We're dressed in nice clothes because Christmas Eve is our cover.
The cathedral in Bà Rịa is packed. If anyone asks why we're out,

we can say we were at Mass. Anyone being the police. The locals
of course recognize us. We stop at one of the popular stalls

for fresh sugarcane juice, trying to act normal. The *nước mía*
tastes unbelievably good. The young woman operating the noisy,

shiny contraption calms us, and when she spots the *Công an*
patrolling out front, insists we sit down and just relax in the back.

Our boat is parked at the riverbank behind the road that runs
past the market, hidden by the lush green flags growing there.

Our third attempt. The last time we waited and waited
at the designated safe house, but no boat ever showed up.

This time we are wiser. My father, thanks to his credentials
as a former Navy officer and ex–reeducation camp prisoner,

negotiated to be boat captain, which means we travel for free—
my mother, my uncle, my cousin, and me—but also means

he can't stay with us because he must collect more passengers
at the bus stop. Say you are devising plans to flee. There's a group,

on Facebook, Asylum and Immigration Without Smugglers,
you can trust and rely on. Because to be a refugee, you must know

where to go, what routes save time and money, if the sea today
or tomorrow is fatally dangerous, if the storm is practically over,

what island is best to leave for, what to do if you are stuck
in the middle of the forest, where to cross the border at night . . .

We have to wait until nightfall. The moon is our lighthouse.
When the time comes, we start walking toward the river

that will lead us to the sea—at this point in my mother's account
a new detail emerges, something small, but not there before:

she loses her sandal like in a fairy tale by mistake in the street.
Because she thinks she sees police lights up ahead, she panics,

hurries in the dark, heart racing, bare foot sparking the path
to the boat motionless and obscure on the river's black mirror . . .

In 1981, the rest of the passengers had to pay two to three
cây vàng, about two to three thousand US dollars then.

I learned that traffickers, in 2014, raised their prices again,
charging at least four thousand dollars to smuggle a Syrian

into Italy. I saw the picture of three-year-old Alan Kurdî
and read one article that tried to describe what his small body

looked like washed ashore, "face down, his head to one side
with his bottom slightly up—the way toddlers like to sleep."

Waiting in the boat's hold, the story goes I won't stop crying.
My crying is an alarm unnerving and endangering everyone.

Because my father is the only one on board who knows how
to pilot the boat and navigate the waters, I am not harmed.

Still, my crying. Incessant, unappeasable, loud as a siren.
My mother doesn't know what to do. She has already fed me

the food she brought. The rice balls, the hard-boiled eggs.
She even tried the sleeping pills. Nothing seems to work.

Though it's risky, she finally carries me up to the deck.
Night air quiets me. Because in my version, her black shawl

covers my head as she hums a song nobody can hear,
all silent, all still, like an island in the Mediterranean.

The epigraph comes from *Absalom, Absalom!* by William Faulkner (Random House, 1936).

"Small Wars" and "A Brief History of Reenactment" were inspired by photographs in An-My Lê's *Small Wars* (Aperture, 2005).

"To a Human Skull" is based on the translation of Chế Lan Viên's poem "Cái Sọ Người" in *An Anthology of Vietnamese Poems: From the Eleventh through the Twentieth Centuries*, edited and translated by Huỳnh Sanh Thông (Yale, 1996).

"Video Elegy" begins with two italicized lines from James Tate's poem "The Lost Pilot."

"Initial Encounter with Locals" incorporates and adapts language found in the *Vietnamese Phrase Book* published by the Department of the Army in July 1962.

"At the Vietnam Center and Archive" draws on the correspondence of Nguyễn Văn Thể in the General Office Files from the Families of Vietnamese Political Prisoners Association Collection at the Vietnam Center and Archive, housed at Texas Tech University. I thank archivist Ann Mallett for leading me to these files.

"Fish in a Well" is a translation of Phan Nhiên Hạo's poem "Cá Trong Giếng," and "Regarding the Spiritual and Social Situation of Vietnam Today" is a translation of his poem "Cảm nhận về tình trạng tinh thần, xã hội Việt Nam hiện nay." Both poems by Phan Nhiên Hạo were originally published in the online journal *litviet*.

"Email from Nguyễn Quốc Chánh" is a translation of "Thư Nguyễn Quốc Chánh," a found poem originally published in Phan Nhiên Hạo's second collection, *Chế Tạo Thơ Ca 99-04* (VĂN, 2004).

"Statue of the Century" is based on the translation, by Nguyễn Ngọc Bích with Burton Raffel and W. S. Merwin, of the poem of the same name by Trụ Vũ, found in *A Thousand Years of Vietnamese Poetry* (Knopf, 1975).

"Lives of the Vietnamese Poets" incorporates and adapts entries on various poets written by Linh Dinh and myself for the Viet Nam Literature Project's Wikivietlit.

"Elsewhere I Don't Know, But Here Must Be Different" is a translation of Nguyễn Quốc Chánh's poem "Ở đậu tao không biết, nhưng ở đây phải khác," originally published in the online Vietnamese journal *Tiền Vệ*.

In "Blackout," the Vietnamese poet alluded to is Chế Lan Viên.

"Events Ashore" was inspired by the photographs of An-My Lê in her monograph of the same title (Aperture, 2014).

"March in Atlanta" is a translation of Phan Nhiên Hạo's poem "Tháng Ba Atlanta," originally published in the online journal *litviet*.

"Greyhound, 1992" is a translation of Phan Nhiên Hạo's poem "Xe buýt 1992," originally published in *Chế Tạo Thơ Ca 99-04* (VĂN, 2004).

"*The Sorrow of War* in Bloomington, Indiana" is a found poem drawn from Bảo Ninh's novel *The Sorrow of War*, translated by Phan Thanh Hao, edited by Frank Palmos (Pantheon, 1994.)

"My Viet Cong" quotes from *The Vietnam War Almanac* by Harry G. Summers, Jr. (Ballantine Books, 1985), Ian Cohen's Pitchfork.com review of the album *Viet Cong* from January 22, 2015, and Virginia Woolf's novel *To the Lighthouse*.

"My Mother Says the Syrian Refugees Look Like Tourists" incorporates and adapts quotations from the *New Yorker*'s October 26, 2015, essay by Nicholas Schmidle entitled "Ten Borders: One Refugee's Epic Escape from Syria."

*

Grateful acknowledgment is made to the editors of the following publications, in which some of these poems first appeared: *Asymptote Journal, Bennington Review, Boston Review, Brooklyn Rail, Cerise Press, diaCRITICS, Drunken Boat, Everyday Genius, Iowa Review, jubilat, Kartika Review, Lana Turner, Matter, New England Review, New Yorker, NOÖ Journal, Poetry, PoetryNow, Prelude, Public Pool, Sink Review, Waxwing, West Wind Review*.

Thank you to the editors of Convulsive Editions, Nate Hoks and Nikki Flores, for publishing a selection of these poems as the chapbook *Small Wars* (2016).

"My Father's *Norton Introduction to Literature*, Third Edition (1981)" was reprinted in *Best American Poetry 2016*, edited Edward Hirsch (Scribner, 2016), and *The Broadview Introduction to Literature*, Second Edition, edited by Lisa Chalykoff, Neta Gordon, and Paul Lumsden (Broadview Press, 2018).

This book would not exist without the generous support of many individuals and institutions.

I am indebted to the National Endowment for the Arts for a literature fellowship that made the completion of this work possible. For invaluable gifts of time, money, and community, I also wish to thank the University of the Florida's Creative Writing Program, Grinnell College and its English Department, and the Bread Loaf Writers' Conference.

To Sarah Gorham and everyone at Sarabande Books for believing in this book and this poet: endless thanks.

Deep gratitude to the friends who read these poems and made them better. Special thanks to Michael Hofmann for taking me under his wing, Linh Dinh for not compromising, Phan Nhiên Hạo for trusting me with his poetry, Jeanette Tran for the years, Mark de Silva for camaraderie, Christie Dam for being there, Andrew Donovan for abiding, Nate Klug for fellowship, my family for patience and sanctuary.

And Roya Biggie, for love and infinite variety.

HAI-DANG PHAN was born in Vietnam in 1980 and grew up in Wisconsin. His work has appeared in the *New Yorker*, *Poetry*, *Best American Poetry 2016*, and the chapbook *Small Wars*. He is the recipient of a National Endowment for the Arts Literature Fellowship, the Frederick Bock Prize from *Poetry*, and the *New England Review* Award for Emerging Writers. He currently teaches at Grinnell College and lives in Iowa City, Iowa. *Reenactments* is his first book.

SARABANDE BOOKS is a nonprofit literary press located in Louisville, KY. Founded in 1994 to champion poetry, short fiction, and essay, we are committed to creating lasting editions that honor exceptional writing. For more information, please visit sarabandebooks.org.